Rhapsodies and Musings

~ poets in the mirrors of other eyes ~

Ketaki Datta and Tania Chakravertty

HAWAKAAL PUBLISHERS

Published by: **Hawakaal Publishers**, 185, Kali Temple Road, Nimta, Calcutta 700049, India.

Printed at: Shanti Mudran, Pataldanga Street, Calcutta 700009.

Contact: Bitan Chakraborty

Email: hawakaal.pb@gmail.com

Cell: + 91 9088029197

1st edition (India): July, 2015
Cover design: Partha Pratim Das
ISBN-13: 978-81-931666-6-6 [Paperback]

Price: INR Two hundred and twenty five only (Rs. 225/- only)

Publisher's Note

We have been planning to get into the world of English literature for some time now, and we could not afford to refuse the proposal that came our way. Two Indian English poets of much esteem: Sharmila Ray and Kiriti Sengupta! Two eminent critics: Ketaki Datta and Tania Chakravertty!! All of them are based in Kolkata. Nothing else could have been more gratifying than publishing *Rhapsodies and Musings*, a book on literary criticism. And with this collection we step into the world of publication of English-language books. We highly intend to cross the language barrier and reach out to the world readers of English literature. We are extremely happy and grateful to the authors, and we consider ourselves privileged from being associated with such a brilliant literary work that, we believe, will be cherished by the readers, researchers and critics across the globe!

Bitan Chakraborty

Founder, Hawakaal Publishers, Kolkata.

Critical acclaim for Sharmila Ray

Sharmila Ray's "Losing Color" is an exploration of a desolate and fractured existence with slender possibility of hope — *The Hindu Literary Review*

The tranquil sounds of seawater crashing on a gravelly beach, is reflected through her [Sharmila Ray's] language of poetry, which perhaps attempts to heal ailing souls and preserve what is worth preserving — *The Statesman*

Sharmila Ray has already carved a niche for herself as an established Indian English poet — *Muse India*

Sharmila Ray always seems suspended between vision and reality. Simplicity of expression is an important aspect of Ray's verse — *Indian Literature*

Rhapsodies of Sharmila Ray: And My Musings

Ketaki Datta

Between my finger and my thumb

The squat pen rests; snug as a gun.

—"Digging" by Seamus Heaney

Sharmila Ray is not a very new name in the circle of poets in India. Basically an academic with a solid background in History as a subject, Sharmila dovetailed her profession with her passion: poetry. After graduating from Presidency College, with a major in History, she fell in love with painting and held several painting exhibitions at different nooks of this metropolis, Kolkata, with her canvases, in an array. Later, while working in City College, Sharmila wooed her former love: poetry and still it is on. She says, "On reaching sixty, I shall paint again. For the nonce, let it take a backseat."

I came to know, Sharmila Ray, when she had been invited to a college, off Calcutta, to speak on "poetry." I was invited there too. I was readily sucked into her deliberations, when she said, "We all have a Disneyland somewhere, tucked away at the corner of our hearts, almost unknowingly. But, once we are out on quest, it opens up its beauty in front of our eyes and we, like possessed souls, keep on following the muse and continue writing poems or color blank canvases or reciprocate with our creativity in some other way. The honeymoon period passes on to intimacy with the afflatus and our creation goes on till we are under the mesmerism. Though I used to write poems occasionally, I never had thought so seriously about writing poems. Especially about finding a wonderland inside our hearts, lying unexplored!" Immediately, I thought of reading more of her poems. And, before parting, she had given me a copy of her lately published book of poems titled "With Salt and Brine" [Yeti Books, July, 2013]. I found Keki Daruwalla's comment on the back cover:

> Not many poets have the gumption to venture into long poems these days, (mea culpa). That Sharmila Ray has gone about it with such élan is truly a surprise. While on the one hand it looks like a free-floating poem, she has yet managed to keep a tight control over it. A fine and enjoyable read.

On the train, I finished reading the 100 four-lined poems the book was composed of, and, was left with a feeling of looking for an answer to the riddles of my being here on earth, gauging my existence with a yardstick which will lead me on to a philosophical understanding of the universe! I was absorbed in the vortex of such an intriguing experience, that, I wanted to know the poet more. I sought an appointment with her, met her and we talked at length on her creation. She opened up, I found an 'aleph', cocooned somewhere in her soul.

Before I talk about her poems why not deal with the definition of a 'poet'? "A poet is an unacknowledged legislator of the world," Shelley opined in his "A Defence of Poetry" (1821).To quote Shelley again in this regard:

> On a Poet's lips I slept/Dreaming like a love-adept/In the sound his breathing kept;/Nor seeks nor finds he mortal blisses,/ But feeds on the aerial kisses/ Of shapes that haunt Thought's wildernesses./He will watch from dawn to

gloom/ The lake- reflected sun illume/ The yellow-bees in the ivy-bloom,/ Nor heed nor see what things they be—/But from these create he can/ Forms more real than living Man,/ Nurslings of Immortality. ["The Poet's Dream" by P. B. Shelley]

Imagination, thus, matters the most with a poet of the Romantic era. But, Shelley talks about the poets of all times, who depends on the faculty of Imagination in order to add 'strangeness to beauty'. To Wordsworth, "a poet is a man speaking to men" [cf. Preface to *Lyrical Ballads*]. To the modern readers, a poet is a go-between in a society among individuals, where the people do not have any time to sit back and relax and scrape friendship with others. Sharmila Ray's poems echo many a modern poet, though, she has an appeal of her own. Poets are on the increase with each passing day, poems equally are so. I do not question their accuracy as "poems," I do not even question the creativity of a "true" poet. Again, I am not at all at one with Plato's risible though horrendous declaration of banishing the poets. My intention is crystal clear. I try to posit Sharmila logically in a frame, which she fits into.

Sharmila Ray is basically an academic with a doctorate in History. An alumnus of Presidency College and Calcutta University, presently she is an Associate Professor and Head of the department of History at City College, Kolkata. Since the last twenty years she is into poetry-writing. She hails from a family of dilettante: her uncle, father's elder brother, Manindra Ray, to whom she dedicates her latest book *With Salt and Brine*, was a Sahitya Award winning poet, her brother, Ananya Ray, who had an early demise was a poet of considerable renown too. Poetry runs in her family, gushes in her blood. She has five books of poetry to her credit, apart from the already-mentioned *With Salt and Brine.* They are: *Earth Me and You* (Granthalaya, Kolkata, 1996), *A Day with Rini* (Poetry and Art, 1998), *Down Salt Water*(Poets Foundation, Kolkata, 1999), *Living Other Lives* (Minerva Press, New Delhi, Mumbai, London, 2004), *It's Fantasy, It's Reality* (Punascha, Kolkata, 2010). She has even tried to wed music (sarod: an Indian string instrument) to poetry and has been successful in bringing out a CD titled *Journey through Poetry and Music.* For some time she was in charge of the column *Moving Hand Writes* (Cal Times, Times of India). She also edited *Poetry and Art,* a journal of poetry and art (1992- '98) and *The Journal* (2012-'13), a poetry journal of the Poetry Society of India. Presently, she is the editor of *Poetry and Prose.* A remarkable point to add here, the book cover of *Living Other Lives* had been designed by the world-famous artist M.F. Hussain, who did it spontaneously, being won over by the magic and charm of Sharmila Ray's poems.

Such a formal introduction is not enough to know the poet thoroughly. Making foray into her poems would be the best way to know Sharmila Ray as a poet of the modern era. In a poem, "Words," Sharmila tells us how she juggles with "words" with which she constructs her poems:

> Alphabets jumble words mingle
> as I start writing a poem.
> Long lines of words.
> As I go on talking to you

they are words compressed...
And words have colors too-
Coral, topaz, cerulean.
Words breathe, words speak.
Sometimes, dust settles on words
and they become heavy, engraving on hearts.
But when words loose sound
and become deep seas within us,
then the secrets of the universe
are told in whispers.

And, in another similar poem, "Alphabets" she says, alphabets are words in their rudimentary form, or it would be more apt to say, that, "Alphabets mother of words." And, in a poetic way, she relates to the readers, how alphabets form a word and how intermittently that happens:

Alphabets march to enter my heart
But an ancient wind stops them.
They get lost
they die
without forming a word.
However, in the evening they return
with kites
with clouds.

She does not stop here, but, with a brilliant flourish of images, she goes on to paint with her pen-brush how the alphabets assemble to form words and how in the "forest" of the alphabets the poet loses herself and gives birth to her poetry. The travail of creation is ultimately enjoyable to her.

Alphabets mist of my armpits.
Alphabets the cotton stretched
over my breasts.
Alphabets the invisible horizon.
I'm swept.
In the sense-space of my thought
alphabets grow on their own
as do the fern
much like the nail of your fingers. Alphabets mother of
words.
Alphabets word-forest. And if we do loose ourselves
in the forest, it is exactly then
that we find our voice.

Or, she might take a cue from Wordsworth saying,

"To me the meanest flower that blows can give
Thoughts that do often lie too deep for tears."

[Concluding lines of "ODE: Intimations of Immortality
from Recollections of Early Childhood"]

Thus, Sharmila Ray welcomes us to the world of her
creation. She opens up and her life-view stands writ large
on the lines she pens. We know, any great poet is also a
profound philosopher, and, Sharmila Ray has a life-
vision of her own too. For example, she is in search of the
basic truths in her poems, which might return the lost
values, the beauty and meaning to this grisly earth we
inhabit. Sharmila Ray, perhaps unconsciously chimes in
unison with Jayanta Mahapatra, while the latter
emphasizes the need of depicting the truth and only the
truth through a poet's words:

Today
I stand on the bank of the poem,
even though each word has a price,
even though this poetry appears as a river,
a river without water
we have to swim across,
and even if its words
do not welcome us to its secret country
where we live without knowing.

[from *Shadow Space,* 1997, by J. Mahapatra]

While talking about the ruthless murder that claimed the lives of Faisal in Basra or Rumi in Kabul, Sharmila Ray bleeds within and writes:

It Could Be

Faisal shot in Basra
Rumi killed in Kabul
Ayan sick and dead in Kashmir.
I don't want to think of them.
It saddens me. It saddens me to think of them
in their original color.
Yet, I am bound to remember them
and memory turns cold, bent and melts away
only to return larger and fatter
until it joins other dark lines.
...
I don't want to think of them;
Faisal shot in Basra
that could be me
Rumi killed in Kabul

that could be me
Ayan sick and dead
and that could be you.

[From *It's Fantasy, It's Reality*]

In this terror-ridden world, when none knows how the last curtain comes ringing down on one's life, faith in art and poetry can enliven us and can make us enjoy each moment we live on earth. Though in another poem titled "Search," Ray clearly states her search is for "peace," which might have been lost somehow in this day-to-day world of "IMF cheque books, booby traps, fear." She concludes the poem with these meaningful lines, on a positive note:

Search

...I haven't heard of peace
Possibly it lives in some forgotten land.
But still I search.
Perhaps a drop of my blood
Like the first monsoon rain
Will sow peace again.

[From *It's Fantasy, It's Reality*]

Aren't we being reminded of Ben Jonson's lines where he says,

In small proportions we just beauties see;
And in short measures life may perfect be.

["The Noble Nature"]

Once Auden was asked, "Does poetry make anything happen?" His straight answer was a big "No." Theodor Adorno opined that after Auschwitz no poetry could happen. But, we know that poetry survived Auschwitz and cruel times gave birth to forceful lines of poetry, which again reminds us of Bertolt Brecht who asserted that poetry cannot stand still, even in bad times, poetry will be written and it would be poetry of bad times. [Courtesy: "No end to Hope" by K. Satchidanandan, Frontline, column: Through My Window, Jan 24, 2014, p.90] May I bend these words [as mentioned by Satchidanandan] and put them on the first line of Dickens's *A Tale of Two Cities* - "It was the best of times" replaced with "poetry of best times", "it was the worst of times" with "poetry of worst times?" However, the teacher of History makes her presence felt, when she talks about the deplorable plight of the current times and rues aloud in her "Think For A Moment," again an excerpt from *It's Fantasy, It's Reality:*

No monument, no sign
nothing,
not even a crude gravestone
stands over Godhra or Ayodhya
or any such place you can think of.
I am afraid because I'm old in years
I am afraid because I am a nobody
hounded, slandered, usurped
by terrible pogrom boots.

If we take a peep into her latest book of 100 poems, in which 100 pearls seem to get woven into a single long string, we again find the responsible history teacher, who can hardly turn a blind eye to whatever disturbing or significant ensue around her, in her times. Poetry speaks ill of the tyrants from the pages of history, poetry again cries on the altar of justice for the tortured souls of the victims. Poetry clamors for justice as poetry is born out of a "cause." The history teacher in Sharmila Ray pops out in the open, truly, in her book of hundred poems, *With Salt and Brine* [2013]:

No.40.

Suddenly the outline of a landscape emerged
'Third World' we realized at once
as images got projected on LED screen
far from the land of well fed.

No. 41.

Did we give the name 'Third World'
or someone else? We debated a long time,
'Argumentative Indians' that's what we are
viewing life with a strange discourse.

Sharmila Ray, in this newest collection, spews her disgust at the terrorists who pollute the air with their nasty, deadly schemes, eulogizes "books" which are symbols of knowledge representing "power," she upholds the need of all religions for the peace of Universal Soul, she takes a pledge of confirming "promises waiting in" her poems. Peace and love are the two refrains that repeat in her poems in sundry ways, but, cocking a snook at Plato's inane declaration of banning all poets, Sharmila Ray makes us feel that poets are gems of Nature, who come to preach the truth, and live in truth and love and peace. A poet's creation is a viaticum in the journey to Eternity. In poem no. 98, she asserts,

> Like a stone in a fruit
> the poem was inside questions and doubts,
> it flirted with the pigments of nature
> tantalizing eternity.

Sharmila Ray casts equal gaze on contemporary culture, religion, politics, books, poems, art – everything under the sun, in this book of hundred poems, thus, giving us an eclectic delight of her creative exuberance. For example:

No. 37.

> We drank Tom Collins with a lemon twist,
> snacked on tiny peppered potatoes and nuts,
> elsewhere the speakers blared nasal tunes,
> we wondered what happened to Nusrat Fateh Ali Khan.
> [contemporary culture]

No. 42.

> 'Western Gaze' that's what it is
> it leaves the 'Third World' almost matt,
> cities with mechanical eyes
> erase nostalgia with a global air brush. [politics]

No. 58.

> The book traveled from city to city
> in caravan, truck and internet,

blessed were those that welcomed it
free from patriarchs, baptized, reborn. [books]

No. 100.

We moved from shadow into light,
the smell of Frankincense hung heavy in the air,
with hidden jets of russet daybreak
confirmed the promises waiting in our poem. [poem]

No.60.

It had the expanse of a Florentine fresco,
madness of Andy Warhol,
a fleeting Mona Lisa smile made it shimmer,
guarding privacy like a Night Watchman. [art]

No.80.

We prayed deep, deep and deeper still and
there was Christ talking to a smiling Buddha,
while Allah stroked the heavenly fire
in tune with Krishna's flute. [religion]

Even, 'violence and terrorism' that rock the present times
has not been lost sight of. Ironically, says Sharmila Ray,

No. 10.

Smothered in heat by April sun
the city gates reflected copper light,
but what's the use of closed gates
when violence seeps in like virus?

Why not take a look at her brilliant collection of poems titled *Living Other Lives*? She toys with the invisible borderline between stories and memories, the latter of course, is volatile, and again the borderline between the two is tenuous. In a poem "Sense of Loss" from this collection, she says,

.....
So he says stories?
"yes please," she says.
"where were we?"
"we have just entered memories-earth-memories in fact."
The sky opens with speeding cloud
there is no sound only vast sand dunes,
you try to give shape and form
and the stories gush out with special tunes...
Memories, they traverse from Neptune's treasures
to forbidden pleasures, from voids to shouts,
from wholesome images to ice and fragility.
They try to find a city
the city of their desire.
The city exists but it eludes them. It isn't here, over there or somewhere else.
You can't put a tag of time or distance to it.
Yet, the city exists.
They get lost.
Memories upon memories
and the stories soak it up,
They hunt for the city.
The city exists.
A border city between memories and stories.

Lost time like vanished civilizations may be relived in memories, though, the real city might not exist in the contemporary times. But it still exists in 'the realm of memory'. Hence, through the warps and woofs of the stories, memory breathes in a seeming reality, which contains the city intact. According to Shramila Ray, "It is a border city between memories and stories."

Sharmila Ray breaks the line between the poetry and prose, when she dovetails the two in her slim coffee-table volume "A Day with Rini." Here, the book is interspersed with brilliant abstract paintings [by Sudhangshu] of human faces — sometimes a lady painter before her canvas, sometimes juxtaposed faces of a lady and a gentleman against a matt backdrop, sometimes a lady's face in dilemma propped up to meet a man's at askance, and so on. And again, breaking the barriers of poetry and prose, Sharmila Ray makes an easy foray into the world of "dialogues" with Rini, the lady, she is obsessed with. I think, Sharmila Ray has been experimenting with different forms of expression in this volume: poetry, prose, art, dialogues to name a few. Interestingly enough, the dialogues are mostly between an animate and an inanimate or imaginary figure/figures. For example, the dialogue sometimes ensues between Rini and The Other Voice or the Mirror or Moments.

In the tête-à-tête with Moments, Rini points out the viability of the Moments, to which each and every "created," animate object on earth owes much. Moments do not know in the faintest that they are so significant to the inhabitants of earth. While Rini stresses the importance of Moments, the latter gets a feel of its necessity in the life of each living sensate being. The conversation has an immaculateness of some sort with a far more ultimate serious import:

Rini And Moments

Rini: You know these little moments are so meaningful that life gets crucified without them.

Moments: Really! I just thought I was the pink flesh of time and abstract romanticism for lovers.

Rini: How can you think like this? Planted with the first heart beat on this universe, you enliven the conspiracy of silence. How can you forget that you fuel the vibrant experiences of soul and senses?

Moments: You're putting too much value on me. Don't you think I exist in ambiguities and the exploits of language?

Rini: You must be mad. Have you ever thought that solitude, sickness, happiness, sexual experience would be inert forms without you?...

Moments: You mean to say that I'm a sort of a bridge tunneling time, I link hemispheres with sounds, scents and color.

Rini: Now you've got it right. You're that little atom in time, beneath vegetation, gathering shadows and cloudless skies. You're there in the steamed coffee-mug and a bear-hug. You were celebrated with the first communion and fire — a threshold awaiting immediate re-birth.

It is quite interesting to note that, explorations of the inner within of Rini are couched in poetic richness, whatever the form of expression may be. In prose, when Sharmila Ray strives to make Rini's emotions public, she unconsciously or consciously slips into the world of poetry, sublime and surreal. As in here:

> Rini wanted to climb out of herself, climb out forever and bite her way into sheer light, hopspringing centuries, leaving behind the snobbishness of earthly autumns and suspicious growth on heart walls.

> She wanted to enjoy the crunch of leaves underfoot and the heat that ascended summer. She wanted to ferry across constellations where Time would throw up his measuring stick and laugh with her, so that anything and everything would no more be distant than a breath between here and there. [17]

No word can describe the charm of poetry that casts spell on the readers readily, in a trice. To quote a few lines would, I believe, be apt:

Soliloquy

I am lying
lying perhaps for few hours
between sleep and awaking
I find the earth moving,
a huge basket forever spinning
overflowing with mountains
greenfields and of course
miles of laughter, miles...

A Day With Rini is, thus, an exquisite collage of poetry, art, dialogue and prose, the underlying unity being sustained through 'poetic' impulse. A sensitive poet never misses a chance to bring the best out of him/her, but, it depends on the efficiency of one to accomplish it. Sharmila Ray is adept in making all the paths of all genres converge at one point, i.e. poetry.

Sharmila Ray's collection *Down Salt Water* contains quite a few poems where her experiment with words, the poetic cadence and appeal, the images –all talk of her excellence in concealing thoughts behind the sparkle of words. In "And She Stood" and "She II," we can easily feel the "alone-ness" of the lady though she is not "lonely" at all. In the collection *Earth, Me and You,* a poem "Autumn of Antiquity," certifies that, the search of the poet for the past in her by "decoding," leaves one mesmerized. In "Love Me," the conundrum lying in the lines: "Love me not again/Love me always..." means a lot, one interpretation being, the transience of everything including "love," which is otherwise bound to be eternal. Hence, "always" reverberates through the lines, leaving the poet determined to mark 'love' as an all-time affair, which has no conclusion, no termination. As already has been mentioned, Sharmila Ray, brings forth her passion for history in her poems like "Oh Alexandria," where she metaphorically deliberates on the ravages of Time, reminding us of Anglo-Saxon elegies like "The Ruined Berg," "The Wanderer,"

...There is no answer.
Under the windswept plain
criss-crossed by archaeologist's digging spree
the city-blood clots

and language turns to hieroglyphs.
Time whitewashes, coat after coat
till the passionate midnights find place
in museum halls.so forth:

History resuscitates the past, leaving an impression on us that we can relive the 'past' if we desire. And, the immediate culprit is none but Time, who cares not for who lives and dies and when the next age starts off on the debris of the previous one. Sharmila Ray toys with words to churn out a flawless picture of the time she lives in. Poetry can make us nostalgic, again, it should leave a message for the readers, so that, apart from enjoying, the reader can derive food for thought for the whole day, may be, for the whole year, nay, for an indefinite period, say, lifetime!

Sharmila Ray's poems leave many a poetry-lover with a sense of fulfillment, an intense desire to live life, an utmost satisfaction of reading. So far as the themes of her poems are concerned, like the metaphysical poets, she has a variety of them; regarding style, she is a matchless craftsman, who can lead a reader straight from the ground we stand upon to the ground realities of life, we often dare not explore so intrepidly. Sharmila Ray is not just a gifted poet but she segues on to writing prose pieces for various national and international journals and even she is an editor of an online prose journal. As here the scope is limited, I resist the temptation of commenting on her prose.

Celebrated poet Jayanta Mahapatra reacted to Sharmila Ray's soul-stirring lines, while he had a chance to comment,

Qualities of tenderness and compassion in s ray's poems set them apart from much of the general flow in current poetics. I did come across technique and craftsmanship, not the sort found in academic journals, but the sort that knows when rules have to be broken, and then break them successfully.

"one feels like a caged animal smelling
the future's breath of singed hair.
But, with the dawn we sport a far-off look
Holding a teacup and behave
As if it's all over
In another land
On another day
Of another era."

Truly, I was somewhat stirred by the spell of these poems.

Even Ashok Vajpayee comments on her debut poetical work:

Sharmila Ray is a new voice young, restless ... The poetry is deeply rooted in the ordinary day-to-day living but reaches out to that which is subterranean, which lies beyond the obvious ... Sharmila Ray carves out a place, a modest space, for herself with dreams glistening in the eyes and words drenched in passionate tension.

In gamut, Sharmila Ray's poems connect "here and now" with the realm beyond this world of day-to-day reality, her poems weave words which are apt, magical, expressive of particular emotions, and, leave room for multiple meanings, which in turn make her poems more modern than they are. In fact, while commenting on his own poem, *The Love Song of J. Alfred Prufrock,* T.S. Eliot said, "as for the meaning of the poem as a whole, it is not exhausted by any single explanation, for the meaning is what the poem means to different readers."[112] [Quoted in Woodhead, Chris.ed. *Nineteenth and Twentieth Century Verse: An Anthology of Sixteen Poets,* OUP, Hong Kong, 1984.]. Hence, I ask the poetry-lovers of the world to go through Sharmila Ray's poems and to find new and newer meanings, matching their own perceptions of them.

Works Cited

1. Jones, Edmund, D. ed. *English Critical Essays,* S. Publications, Delhi, Asia, 1990.

2. Satchidanandan. K. "No End to Hope," Column: Through My Window in *Frontline,* January 24, 2014. Chennai, India.

3. Woodhead, Chris. ed. Nineteenth and Twentieth Century Verse: An Anthology of Sixteen Poets, OUP, Hong Kong, 1984.

4. Davies, Walford, ed. *William Wordsworth: Selected Poems,* J.M. Dent & Sons, 1975.

5. Different works of Sharmila Ray.

About Ketaki Datta

Dr. Ketaki Datta is an Associate Professor of English, Bidhannagar College, Kolkata. She is a novelist, short story writer, critic and a translator. She had been to Lisbon on an invitation from IFTR [Ireland chapter] to read out a paper titled "Human Values and Modern Bengali Drama," which got published in *The Statesman* in India. *Indo-Anglian Literature: Past to Present* [2008], *New Literatures in English: Fresh Perspectives* [2011], *Avenel Wings of Short Fiction* [2012], *Selected Short Stories of Rabindranath Tagore in Translation* [2013], *The Black and Nonblack Shades of Tennessee Williams* [2012], *The Last Salute* [Sahitya Akademi, 2013], *The Voyage* [2009], *Across The Blue Horizon* [poetry collection, England, 2014], and two novels [*A Bird Alone* (2008) and *One Year for Mourning* (2014)] are a few of her notable publications. Her short story has been published in *New Asian Writing Anthology*, 2013. She is the only contributor from India in the forthcoming book titled *Routledge Companion to Dramaturgy*, being compiled by Prof. Magda Romanska of Emerson College, Boston, USA.

Critical acclaim for Kiriti Sengupta

Sengupta's short poems like "Celluloid," "Fish Lip," and "Memorandum Of Understanding" mirror the Japanese Haikus, grasping the mystery and miracle of life in a cryptic idiom – *The Hindu Literary Review*

Keats once said famously, "If poetry comes not as naturally as the leaves to a tree it had better not come at all." For Kiriti, poetry comes naturally as does the prose pieces accompanying his poetic effusions – *Muse India*

The poetic vision he [Sengupta] lends to his experiences and deep meditation on things we take for granted in our indifferent stride, shakes up our mental lethargy and prods us to reflect intensely on such matters – *The Fox Chase Review and Reading Series*

A pioneering genius in poeticizing yogic science, Dr. Kiriti emerges as a rare poet. Through yogic poetry, he has dared to tread the inexplicable labyrinthine path of literature that only the literate few would dare do – *Contemporary Vibes*

Rhapsodies of Kiriti Sengupta: And My Musings

Tania Chakravertty

Dr. Kiriti Sengupta and I became acquainted roughly a year and a half back. A friend of mine, an eminent academician, told me over the phone that he wanted me to join him for the launch of two books; one purely a collection of Bengali poems by Shri Ranadeb Dasgupta, and the other, a collection of poems by Smt. Sumita Nandi accompanied by translations by Dr. Kiriti Sengupta. Smt Nandi and Dr. Sengupta handed me their volume of verses on the day we first met and the book launch happened as per schedule about a month later.

Even after more than a year of acquaintance, I admit, I didn't know that Dr. Sengupta was a poet himself, along with being translator, writer of non-fiction, editor and interviewer. Just about a month back, he presented me with a copy each of his literary endeavours and pursuits. Sengupta's literary endeavours are all the more noteworthy because he is a dental surgeon by profession occasionally having forays into the world of literature.

My Glass of Wine

Some of Sengupta's poems that I am going to critique are from this collection titled *My Glass of Wine*. I found this collection a little offbeat because each of the poems is preceded by a short prose piece that introduces the subject, theme and the context of the poem involved. Readers might wonder why. Would not too much of explanation, too much of contextualization on the poet's part take away the mysticism involved with the genre of poetry itself? Sengupta's contextualization is meticulous and he takes care not to spoil the reader's interest with mere facts and figures. He provides us with the background story associated with each poem because his poems are "personal" poems. Without the personal context, the true meanings of the poems might remain incomprehensible. As Don Martin states in the foreword, Sengupta in *My Glass of Wine* is essentially interviewing himself.

In the Preface, Sengupta reveals his reluctance to accept the categorisation of "Indian-English" writers, a categorisation meted out by literary scholars that he himself falls under. He reminds his readers that English, after all is not a foreign language in India. English is an international language and is predominantly used in all formal affairs. He boldly states that writing in English is "just a matter of personal choice" (19) reminding the reader yet again, that the English language is very much a part of Indian cultural values, just as the numerous vernacular ones. In this context I am reminded of Arjun Appadurai's arguments on the concept of culture. Appadurai states, "General definitions of culture rightly cover a lot of ground ranging from general ideas about human creativity and values, to matters of collective identity and social organization, matters of cultural integrity and property, and matters of heritage, monuments and proportions" (Appadurai 76). Taking English to be a part of the Indian multi-cultural framework, Sengupta states that he thinks in English too before he writes unlike many Indians and adds that as a poet he "speaks his mind" (20) not bothered about the effect. Yet, Sengupta hopes that readers will enjoy the "distinct images," (20) and the "shreds of autobiographic images" (26) that he has chosen from his life.

In "As I Traversed," Sengupta speaks of his first encounter with Bengali literature via his girlfriend. He analyses the genre of poetry where he first claims that, "Poetry may prove to be captivating, enchanting, melodious, rhythmic and fantasizing, but can never entertain in the first place," (33) and then Sengupta contradicts himself as the analysis continues. Since he writes personal poems, he talks about "consuming" the fuel of his being for a good outcome. The poem "Consumption" follows his argument. He writes:

Consumed time
like an infant consuming
milk; inevitable
it remains.
Killed essence of
the eternal soul; and consumed,
essentially I remain... (34)

If Sengupta were to follow T.S. Eliot's dictum that true art should be impersonal, what would that lead to? The clash of opinions still persists – that between the romantic school and the modernist school – Sengupta adheres to the romantic school of thought. It's the creator's choice and I guess it's right for him because if he were to turn impersonal, that would take away the essence of his signature poems, the unique subjective and personal elements. In fact, with the image of the infant who consumes milk, the only food for all infants, Sengupta stresses on the inevitability and spontaneity of his poetic outbursts.

"My Glass of Wine" refers to Sengupta's eagerness to be formally baptized at the behest of a friend when he was a student of Dentistry. As I read this poem I felt that after all this is the picture of India – liberal and secular. He remembers the Reverend Father's suggestion of a "spiritual baptism" and then his initiation to wine, symbolic of the blood of Christ. Sengupta writes:

> I was desperate. I closed my eyes and will full concentration I urged, "Oh Jesus! I am inviting you to come in, and be my savior." I fail to remember what had happened next. All I can remember now is this: I felt some unique sensation within, there was a mild headache, and I had interestingly tender eyes. (38)

The unique sensation he refers to is "epiphanic." The word "epiphany" originally had associations with the divine; it referred to a spiritual insight. The novelist James Joyce contributed much in secularizing this term.

The Joycean epiphany has been defined as "a sudden spiritual manifestation, whether from some object, scene, event, or memorable phase of the mind — the manifestation being out of proportion to the significance or strictly logical relevance of whatever produces it." (Beja, 18).

In the poem "Blood Related" as in the prose introduction "My Glass of Wine," Sengupta refers to his initiation to wine, soon after. He writes:

It was not branded, but a homemade
wine.
Intimately divine,
I drank it first
right after I was spiritually baptized. (40)

In *The Bible*, wine represents God's covenant in blood, poured out in payment for mankind's sin. Jesus Christ says, "This cup is the new covenant in my blood, which is poured out for you" (*Luke* 22:20). Christ wanted people to drink wine as a symbol of His shed blood. The drinking of wine, he knew, would leave an indelible mark on the minds of His followers of His death for the sins of humanity. He states, "This do, as often as you drink it, in remembrance of Me" (1 *Corinthians* 11:25).

Sengupta continues:

You and I
The Father and Son
the legacy goes on.
Inevitable-impeccable,
blood relation... (40)

The poem gathers more meaning with these lines. After all, Christ wanted people to understand that His blood makes it possible for all humans to come before the throne of God. Under the old covenant, only the priest could enter the area of the tabernacle known as the "Holiest of All" (*Hebrews* 9:6-10). It was referred to as the "mercy seat," which represented God's throne. The book of *Leviticus* mentions a ceremony that took place each year on the Day of Atonement, when the high priest sprinkled the blood of a goat, representing the future sacrifice of Jesus Christ, on the mercy seat so the Israelites could be symbolically cleansed of all their sins (*Leviticus* 16:15-16). As the blood of Jesus Christ has cleansed us and made us pure, each person, believe devout Christians, enjoys direct access to the Father (Hebrews 9:24). Each human can approach God without hesitation or fear of rejection because of the blood of Jesus Christ (*Hebrews* 10:19-22).

In "My Glass of Wine" Sengupta refers to similarities of thought, and rituals, in tantric cults of Hinduism and Islam too, where animal sacrifices are mentioned. I have a rather long quote from Jessie Weston's book *From Ritual to Romance* that explains the meanings behind religious rituals. Weston writes:

> Cumont in his *Les Religions Orientalesdans le Paganisme Romain*, speaking of the influence of the Mysteries upon Christianity, remarks acutely, "Or, lorsqu'onparle de mystčres on doitsonger ŕ I'Asiehellénisée, bien plus qu'ŕ la Grčcepropre, malgré tout le prestige qui entourait Eleusis, car d'abord les premičrescommunautés Chrétiennes

se font fondées, formées, développées, au milieu de populations Orientales, Sémites, Phrygiens, Egyptiens.

This is perfectly true, but it was not only the influence of milieu, not only the fact that the 'hellenized' faiths were, as Cumont points out, more advanced, richer in ideas and sentiments, more pregnant, more poignant, than the more strictly 'classic' faiths, but they possessed, in common with Christianity, certain distinctive features lacking in these latter.

If we were asked to define the special characteristic of the central Christian rite, should we not state it as being a Sacred meal of Communion in which the worshipper, not merely symbolically, but actually, partakes of, and becomes one with, his God, receiving thereby the assurance of eternal life? (The Body of Our Lord Jesus Christ preserve thy body and soul unto everlasting life.)

But it is precisely this conception which is lacking in the Greek Mysteries, and that inevitably, as Rohde points out: "The Eleusinian Mysteries in common with all Greek religion, differentiated clearly between gods and men, einsist der Menschen, einandres der Götter-Geschlecht— enandron, entheongenos." The attainment of union with the god, by way of ecstasy, as in other Mystery cults, is foreign to the Eleusinian idea. As Cumont puts it "The Greco-Roman deities rejoice in the perpetual calm and youth of Olympus, the Eastern deities die to live again." [6] In other words Greek religion lacks the Sacramental idea. (Weston)

The ancient civilizations had a profound understanding of human psychology. Does not Carl Jung talk about the collective unconscious of humans irrespective of race and religion? Sacrifices often involving blood of animals or humans were made in the ancient world. The person offering the sacrifice felt that the gods would be appeased and offer something in exchange of the sacrifice. Regarding this issue, Jung states:

> Christ effectively took this torment upon himself and taught them: "Be crafty like serpents and guileless like doves." For craftiness counsels against chaos, and guilelessness veils its terrible aspect. Thus men could take the safe middle path, hedged both upward and downward. (Jung, 300-301)

In this context, I may add, Kenneth Burke first coined the word "scapegoat mechanism" which was developed by René Girard. Humans are driven by mimetic desire, says Girard, desire for that which another desires too or already possesses. This causes conflict between the desiring parties. This mimetic *contagion* puts society at risk and it is at this point that the *scapegoat mechanism* is generated. Gerard argues how sacrificial violence forms a part of all human cultures. The scapegoat mechanism is the means by which a group transfers its collective hostility onto a single victim, killing it/him and returning the group to unity and complacency. Girard recognizes Jesus Christ too as an innocent scapegoat who completes a slow process begun in the Hebrew Bible. The New Testament eventually reverses the violent psychosocial mechanism upon which human culture has been founded. Jesus Christ stops the perpetuation of violence by abstaining from violent retribution.

"My Sister's Bhaiya" brings in the issue of names. Sengupta claims that he has not seen a single Christian bearing the name "Jesus" and adds that naming children after gods and goddesses is a common practice amongst Hindus. I have not seen anybody with the name of Jesus either. As for Hindus, the practice has not been a consistent one. It has happened only in certain periods and sometimes only amongst certain classes.

In the poem "Namesake" Sengupta writes:

> Whispers the tale of your character,
> color and its fragrance merge to call it
> a Rose.
> A lot matters,
> if you remember
> the name... (44)

The image of the rose inevitably reminds us of Shakespeare but the context here is so very different. Sengupta keeps referring to objects in this poem, each of which has a cognition with another object or a particular feeling. The rose reminds us of its fragrance and color; *Nadia Talkies* a theatre hall reminds a boy of the movies watched with delight long after the hall is demolished; the water sac in the womb reminds one of childbirth; crucifixion reminds one of Christ.

38

"Southern Affiliation" deals with Sengupta's trysts with Chennai, erstwhile known as Madras, Udupi and Hyderabad. Sengupta opines that Chennai, "exudes joy, excitement, culture, traditional values, professional excellences, and many more!"

In the poem, "The Encyclopedia," Sengupta writes:

> Since period unknown
> you spin, and continue to swivel;
> you have such firm grip. (50)

Chennai, laden with history, becomes the repository of unending knowledge.

In "Market," Sengupta states:

> ... all those wise people;
> they spread love, and
> receive God.
> They hate the sin... (52)

Udupi, the temple town, becomes the emblem of Indian hospitality, something Indians have prided themselves on since time immemorial.

"Clarity" deals with a simple issue, the preparation of ghee or clarified butter. The poet says:

> I have seen my mother
> preparing Ghee out of milk
>
> ...
> The smell was so organic... (55)

The ghee becomes emblematic of the mother's love –
pure, divine and unadulterated.

The prose section titled "Rains" addresses situations
which are overwhelming; he deals with feelings that
drench the entire being.

In "The Air," the narrator confesses:

> No one knew I worshipped you
> with my flaming heart (60)

Love, indeed, is a feeling that permeates the entire being;
mind and heart, body and soul.

Sengupta, claims that love instead of being volatile, is a
strong cerebral affair. As a medical practitioner he
dispassionately states that after all, "It is the brain, which
governs the heart…" Yet love, touches and leaves a mark,
as he writes in "Scratches Only Are Human":

> Few beautiful scratches, deep within,
> soft marks, palpable even after months;
> no wounds, but tiny scratches brown– (61)

The scratches are somewhat personified, they are given
the attributes of seeing, smiling, talking and capturing
his entire being.

"Stay Away" deals with a refrain with slight changes in
each paragraph; changes which denote different facets
of loving and trying to possess the beloved.

Feeling you wonderfully inside
never fails
...
Feeling you beautifully inside
had been my dream
...
Feeling you humanly inside
is indeed a nightmare (62)

Well, as Coleridge stated (about poets, not about love), love "described in *ideal* perfection, brings the whole soul of man into activity, with the subordination of its faculties to each other, according to their relative worth and dignity." (Coleridge, Chapter IV)

"Clips" is a section with embracing myriad moods. The first bunch of poems talks of love and its various aspects. "In Tune" refers to the harmony achieved in a serious love affair; "Coming Home" deals with love's longings:

In the one I put
my gold, wealth, and all
The other has you, the deity,
and my childhood call. (69)

"Vermillion" sums up the lover's feelings in one beautiful line: "... as I find you eyesome."(69)

In "The Odd Number" Sengupta carefully and subtly deals with narcissistic self-love.

...And the nauseating smell that
Spreads from the blanket damp.

...
solitary in thy conjugal camp. (71)

Certain words draw one's attention to a kind of release, which is not narrated in the text. Filling in the textual gap, one gets to understand that how the lover relieves and pacifies himself.

"My Master and the Cover" is a section devoted to Sengupta's spiritual Guru, who has been named in the text, Dr. Ashoke Kumar Chatterjee, a World Kriyayoga Master who was conferred the title of *Yogacharya*. In the poem, "The Scripture," Sengupta writes:

> Open your heart, and
> use your brain;
> you will reach beyond
> the humanly plane.
> Act your actions,
> mind His name;
> God only dwells
> within mortal frame! (77)

It is a simple rendition of how one may wholeheartedly embrace Yoga. This is followed by the poem "Initiation" which deals with his initiation into Yoga through his *Guru*. He meticulously refers to the Chakras or energy points or knots in the human body that the master / Guru touches and transforms. The initiated exults by saying:

> I fell in love with myself,
> with the sole existence. (78)

Indeed! The goal of a Yogi is not just the controlling the body and the mind. Through Yoga, an individual not only attains holistic health; the human enjoys a direct communion with the Almighty.

References

All references to the primary text are taken from Sengupta, Kiriti. *My Glass of Wine*. New Delhi: Author's Empire. 2013.

Works Cited

Appadurai, Arjun. "The Capacity to Aspire: Culture and the Terms of Recognition." *Culture and Public Action*. Eds. Vijayendra Rao, and Michael Walton. Stanford: Stanford University Press, 2004.

Beja, Morris. *Epiphany in the Modern Novel*. Seattle: University of Washington Press, 1971.

Websites Cited

Coleridge, Samuel Taylor. *BiographiaLiteraria*. Project Gutenberg's Etext. 15 July, 2015. <http://www.gutenberg.org/files/6081/6081-h/6081-h.htm#link2HCH0014>

Jung, Carl. *The Red Book*. 15 July, 2015. <http://carljungdepthpsychology.blogspot.in/2013/10/the-hanging-of-victim-on-tree-was.html>

Weston, Jessie L. *From Ritual to Romance*. The Project Gutenberg E-text. 15 July, 2015. <http://www.gutenberg.org/cache/epub/4090/pg4090-images.html>

The Reverse Tree

This chapter is focused on *The Reverse Tree* which the author categorizes as "non-fiction." I choose to focus on this particular book in the second chapter because, here too, the non-fictional pieces are sometimes followed by little snippets of poems. Gopal Lahiri says that all the six chapters in the book:

> ... are imaginatively inventive to understand the meaning of life. Each chapter represents the working out of a single idea of randomness yet the question remains as Sengupta stated in a different context, "How does one get into another being so effortlessly?" ... It's an amalgam of hues and textures, introducing a new dimension to the narrative that is vastly different from the traditional up and down staffs. One of the ways, he's chosen to explore the issues through honest admission, is the skin color/ racial overtone, or gay-sex/ criminal offence, etc. Sometimes his characters are in crisis and chaos but fight back at the end. (Lahiri)

"Anti-Clock" brings in the issue of men being referred to as trees. Sengupta states that since men are expected to be "masculine," and non-flowery (2), the tree metaphor works perfectly at tandem with the concept. For centuries, theorists had argued that gender roles were dictated by nature and biology and thus their qualities were "naturally" associated with the biological female or male. The biologically sexed woman was thereby presumed to be naturally "feminine," the biologically sexed male naturally "masculine," and gender was defined as having fixed and immutable "natural" characteristics. The preeminence of the male in traditional cultures and androcentric orthodox societies is not viewed still as a social construct, but as a natural signs of "civilization," and evolution. So, if a man is expected to be like a tree, firm, rooted, dependable and strong, a woman is expected to include in herself the virtues which Sengupta may refer to as "flowery" I suppose, like softness, compliance, purity, delicacy and the like.

"In Others Shoes" is a little piece eulogising the art of mimicry as sportingly manifested by one of Sengupta's friends. Well, some people do have a superb ability to mimic, skilled in imitating the voices and gestures of others. Care needs to be taken that copying the articulation and mannerism does not hurt anybody's sentiments. Sengupta focuses on the fun aspect of it all.

"Long ... A Metaphor" is an interesting piece focussing on a man, a poet, sporting long hair. He writes about his appearance:

> ... a small earring on his right lobule
> sorry, earring sounds
> girly
> I'll say a stud rather (8)

Sengupta adds:

> I was then looking at his long hair
> tied up at his back... (8-9)

Sengupta's language throws certain subtle hints. Many men detest keeping long hair because they claim that long hair makes them feel like homosexuals. The artist he met could have been one trying to practice psychosexual creativity and artistry.

The poet laments, "I have failed to become a poet miserably..." (9)

Shoshana Felman writes that the challenge, "is nothing less than to 'reinvent' language, to speak not only against, but outside of the specular phallogocentric structure, to establish a discourse the status of which would no longer be defined by the phallacy of masculine meaning." (Quoted in Showalter 253). The physical manifestations of his artistry and his ambiguous sexual orientation fail to find place amidst the heteronormative order.

"Crisis" is yet another section concerning the third gender. Sengupta reminds us that ancient India was far progressive in thoughts and temperament because Hindu scriptures refer clearly to the *Tritiya Prakriti*, the third sex, along with *Purush*/ male, and *Stree* / female. In fact, Hindu myths constantly refer to the fluidity of gender role playing even by the Gods — Vishnu becoming a female deity as Mohini for example and also begetting a son. The fluidity of gender roles and androgynous selfhood culminates in the image of the *Ardhanarishwara*. The prose section relates the story of Lara, born male, yet with the soul of a female who underwent sex change, and was jilted by an Indian boyfriend. Sengupta writes a poem encapsulating the pang of separation. It says:

gold is precious and so was the time
we spent together; right from the morning tea
spanning over the lavish lunch until you said,
"signing off for today"
I was hesitant, you know,
I never said goodbye. (19)

Countless Indian gay men cheat on their families. Many don't admit to their parents about their homosexual orientations and even marry straight heterosexual women making the lives of their spouses miserable as well. Sengupta documents the terrible agony of Lara who, benumbed with the sorrow of separation, drops out of the university and becomes a sex-worker instead. My mind gets drawn to the suffering of Lara as well as the poor suffering wife who married this man Sumit ignorant about his real nature.

The final section "The Reverse Tree" is interesting because the author picks up certain *slokas*/verses from *The Srimad Bhagavad Gita* and gives them a secular and modern reading. Sengupta speaks of the immortality of the soul and then turns his attention to the role of the Enlightened Master or Guru. Certain teachings of *The Gita* are actually used in modern classrooms in Indian business schools. Shri Krishna acts as what the modern world calls a counsellor when Arjuna faces the dilemma leading to excruciating mental pain. M.P. Bhattathiry writes:

> *The Bhagavad Gita*, written thousands of years ago, enlightens us on all managerial techniques leading us towards a harmonious and blissful

state of affairs in place of the conflict, tensions, poor productivity, absence of motivation and so on, common in most of Indian enterprises today – and probably in enterprises in many other countries. The modern (Western) management concepts of vision, leadership, motivation, excellence in work, achieving goals, giving work meaning, decision making and planning, are all discussed in *The Bhagavad Gita*. (M.P. Bhattathiri)

Bob Miglani, a senior director in Pfizer and author of *Treat Your Customer* states that lessons in leadership contained in *The Bhagavad Gita* are being applied widely in corporate America. Professor Srikumar Rao, who has taught it at Columbia Business School, the London Business School and the Haas School of Business at Berkley also states:

> In the Indian tradition, you are taught action is in our control, but the outcome/goal is out of our hands. I encourage executives to invest completely in the process and not the goal. If they invest every fiber of their being into the process they are likely to enjoy the outcome. It is a paradox. When you become detached from the outcome, strangely enough the probability of achieving the goal rises dramatically ... Good leaders are selfless, take initiative, and focus on their duty rather than obsessing over outcomes or financial gain. (Quoted in Choudhury)

The Gita talks about cause and effect, referred to as karma, and also mentions *nishkam karma* that can be achieved through transcendence of the self-leading to self-realization. Rao uses *The Bhagavad Gita* and other ancient texts to guide business school graduates to self-improvement and corporate enlightenment. He says that he encourages executives to invest completely in the process and not the goal.

Sengupta refers to "a single teacher who has shaped [him] and [his] life" and as a touching tribute, he mentions his mother. That a mother's love is selfless and undemanding is universally accepted and it is this selflessness in mother-love that is in tune with what *The Gita* also preaches. Towards the end of the chapter, Sengupta refers to one *sloka* in *The Gita* that implies the reverse tree:

urdhva-mulamadhah-sakham
asvatthamprahuravyayam
chandamsiyasyaparnani
yas tam vedasaveda-vit (34)

An amazing phenomenon, mentions *The Gita* that humans are trees that have their roots i.e. the brain up, and the branches i.e. the limbs down. Sengupta tries to fathom the beauty and mystery of being human.

References

All references to the primary text are taken from Sengupta, Kiriti. *The Reverse Tree*. Ahmedabad: Moments Publication. 2014.

Works Cited

Showalter, Elaine, ed. *The New Feminist Criticism: Essays on Women, Literature and Theory*. London: Virago, 1986.

Websites Cited

Bhattathiri, M.P. *Bhagavad Gita and Management*. 15 July, 2015.
<http://www.themystica.com/mystica/articles/b/bhagavad_gita_and_management.html>

Choudhury Uttara. *Business Schools Take On Indian Philosophy*. 15 July, 2015.
<http://www.braingainmag.com/business-schools-are-embracing-indian-philosophy.htm>

Lahiri, Gopal. "Understanding the existence of mankind: A reverse approach". *Muse India*. Issue 62: Jul-Aug 2015. 15 July, 2015.
http://museindia.com/regularcontent.asp?issid=61&id=5792 >

Healing Waters Floating Lamps

This chapter concerns *Healing Waters Floating Lamps*, a book of Sengupta which is entirely devoted to poetry. As I browsed through *Healing Waters Floating Lamps*, I found a few poems which appear in other collections too. The collection deals with multifarious aspects of India and what I may call Indian spirituality. Ananya S Guha states in a review, "The voice is always quiet, meditative, it is never sentimental or maudlin. If there is a cry for God, then it is an act of surrender. In fact surrender is one of the dominant themes of these poems. But it precludes any kind of overt religiosity." (Guha)

Many of the poems revolve around the River Ganges or Ganga. *The Bhagavat Purana* says that Ganga was born out of Vishnu's lotus feet, hence her name *Vishnupadi* and thus the river is worshipped as a goddess and considered holy by millions of Hindus. Sengupta writes much about Varanasi too, a city that Mark Twain considered, "older than history, older than tradition, older even than legend, and looks twice as old as all of them put together."

"Beyond The Eyes" tells a simple tale of a devotee who writes:

I reach the sky
While I draw a circle in the water

Looking at the image

I take a dip (3)

A dip in the Ganges is considered holy. As Hindus bathe in the waters of the Ganges, they often pay homage to their forefathers by cupping the water in their hands, lifting it and letting it fall back and by the method described so beautifully in the poem.

"After Bath" naturally follows "Beyond the Eyes." Closely associated with the holy dip is the homage paid to the Sun god through the *Gayatri Mantra*. The poem runs:

> I've bathed your feet with the water of the Ganges
> Last dip in the afternoon, and
> I paid my first obeisance
> ...
> O Sun, I remember
> I've bathed your feet with the water of the
> Ganges... (5)

The *Gayatri Mantra* is intimately associated with the Sun. The invocation concludes with an appeal to illumine our minds and bestow upon us true knowledge. Goddess Gayatri in the myths the consort of Brahma and is also called "Veda-Mata" or the Mother of *The Vedas - Rigveda, Yajurveda, Saamveda* and *Atharvaveda*. Thus as she is hailed along with the sun, the fount of all creativity, the entire universe is paid homage to.

"Evening Varanasi" is a poem I must quote in full. It runs as:

> Have you seen the floating lamps in the river?
> Water here is not the fire-extinguisher, but
> The flames ascend through water
> Prayers reach the meditating Lord (7)

Several places considered holy and sacred by Hindus lie along the banks of the Ganges, including Varanasi. Every evening devotees release candlelit floats into the Ganges with the hope of salvation. This is an age-old tradition. Varanasi is steeped in history, legends and tradition. The city bestows us with a historical sense, giving us, as Eliot says, "a sense of the timeless as well as of the temporal and of the timeless and of the temporal together..." (Eliot)

"In Dusty Feet" has as its theme the very typical Indian practice of *pranam*, where the person paying reverence either prostrates himself/herself in front of the person to whom respect is being paid or touches his/her feet. Touching one's feet has an added implication. It implies that that the person is picking up dust from the feet and placing them on the forehead. Sengupta writes:

> His great toes housed
> Some holy grains of dust
> ...
> And I picked the grains as quickly
> As to place them on my head
> ...
> I wished to become such pious grains
> So as to stay attached with his feet forever ... (15)

In an article, Deepika Birks explains what it means when Hindus touch the feet of elders. She writes, "Foot touching is not done despite feet being considered unclean — it's done because feet are generally considered unclean. It means that the person has walked this earth longer than you and gained such wisdom that you can benefit even from the dust their feet have picked up along the way." (Birks)

"Mellifluous Cry" opens with a labor room drawing our attention first to the midwife, who says Sengupta:

> ... was visibly unhappy with the silence of the newborn
> ...
> The midwife screamed in utter frustration
> "Hey! Cry out." (31)

The beauty of the poem lies in evoking an emotion, that of anticipation, of the father waiting to hear the first cry of the newborn.

> On the other side of the closed door
> The father was eager to hear his baby
> He was all set to smile and celebrate
> The first communication (31)

The poem becomes taut and tense as the poet shows contrasting emotions of the midwife and the father. The poet drops a hint that the baby might be stillborn. But does not the poem also portray an existential angst?

"Give Me More Of Life" involves a young girl, playing with a live fish, not just any fish but a *Koi*.

> A young girl was standing
> At the bank of a river
> Her hands held a live *Koi*
> I was curious, and she said,
> "Hold it and you will understand." (52)

Interestingly, as Sengupta mentions in his footnote, in Bengal, it is said that the life of a boy is delicate and infant boys are considered more fragile and vulnerable as compared to girls. A girl's life is compared to that of a *koi*; infant girls are thought to be able to withstand far more hardships as compared to infant boys. For the narrator, realization comes in a flash, it becomes akin to a beatific vision.

This chapter of mine ends with "Adios" which has as its subject matter the worship of Goddess Durga which is so dear to all Bengalis. Sengupta writes: The mirror has a limited role as we urge, "Please visit us again." (55)

The immersion is actually done in two phases. The *darpan* or the mirror is believed to hold the soul of the mother goddess. The *darpan* is immersed first. After that, with much paraphernalia, the idol is immersed in the Ganga, the body returning to dust as it were.

References

All references to the primary text are taken from Sengupta, Kiriti. *Healing Waters Floating Lamps*. Ahmedabad: Moments Publication. 2015.

Websites Cited

Birks, Deepika. "What does it mean when Hindus touch someone's feet?" *Gathering Nectar*. October 27, 2014. 15 July, 2015.
<http://www.patheos.com/blogs/gatheringnectar/2014/10/what-does-it-mean-when-hindus-touch-someones-feet/

Eliot, T.S. "Tradition and the Individual Talent". 15 July, 2015.
< http://www.bartleby.com/200/sw4.html>

Guha, Ananya S. "Kiriti Sengupta's "*Healing Waters Floating Lamps*" Review" *Literature Studio*. Posted by Vibha Malhotra on Jul 13, 2015 in Book Reviews, General Reading. 15 July, 2015.
http://literaturestudio.in/kiriti-senguptas-healing-waters-floating-lamps-review-by-ananya-s-guha/

Translations
Desirous Water
and
Poem Continuous — Reincarnated Expressions

A few poems that Dr. Kiriti Sengupta has translated into English have appeared in Indian journals of repute like the *Taj Mahal Review* and *Labyrinth,* and in a highly acclaimed international journal published online from Philadelphia, Pennsylvania named *The Fox Chase Review. The Reciting Pens* and *The Unheard I* too bear a couple of poems that he has translated. Sengupta has translated two volumes of poetry, both published in 2014, which I will critique in this chapter.

The first volume *Desirous Water* manifests Sengupta's creativity in the title itself. The poet Ms. Sumita Nandi states in the introduction that her poems are about Icchhemati River. Interestingly, *ichchhe* in Bengali means desire. In my view, Nandi's poems emanate from the river of desire, the river of the unconscious. In a review that I wrote, I claimed:

> For Hélène Cixous, writing becomes the passageway, the entrance, the dwelling place and the exit of the "other" in the woman. The poems of Ms. Nandi made me feel that the libido of woman, her atma, as expressed in *Desirous Water* is cosmic, just as her unconscious; and this is what makes her writing endless and infinite. In compliance with Cixous' demand that women must reject a philosophical mode of writing, Ms. Nandi undermines andro-centric expectations

and demands concerning syntax, grammar and linear thought. She simply writes herself in a fluid language, a specifically feminine discourse. If one were to theorize and pay a feminist attention to her use of language, one would witness the relationship between writing and the poet's body and soul. (Chakravertty)

Actually Cixous asks women to write themselves and make their bodies heard. Only then will the huge resources of the unconscious burst forth, she says. Sengupta's translations effectively portray the poet's unconscious. The male translator effectively manages to portray the woman's emotions, feelings and desires. In some poems, Ms. Nandi uses a male persona too. All of these prove yet again that the mind of the artist is androgynous.

The second volume is titled *Poem Continuous — Reincarnated Expressions*. The poet Bibhas Roy Chowdhury grapples with love and longing for individuals and for humanity at large in poems like "The People," "The Weather Bulletin," "The Connector," "The Debt," and "Poets And Poems." In quite a few poems Roy Chowdhury expresses certain ecological terrors. When crops fail, it leads to the loss of lands by the small farmers. Corporations are formed, and lands begin to be farmed under wide-scale operations. And soon, tractors replace the bullock-drawn ploughs and thus, thousands of small farmers and sharecroppers are rendered worthless. "I Can Leave, But Why?" and "Lunatic" are poems portraying the destruction of mother nature and the plight of the farmers (read as humans)! In quite a few poems like "*Bhatiali* — Song Of The Boatmen," and "The Tie Of Brotherhood," he expresses the angst of countless Bengalis who came over from erstwhile East Bengal, now a separate nation Bangladesh. It is impossible to forget the communal violence that accompanied the Partition of Bengal, which uprooted Bengalis and made them dispossessed and disoriented. The erstwhile bourgeois began to be termed a "refugee." With that alienation came nostalgia. Nostalgia, according to Dipesh Chakraborty, has two aspects, the sentiments and the sense of trauma, and their contradictory relationship to the question of the past. A traumatized memory has a narrative structure which works on a principle opposite to that of any historical narrative. Partition remains a wound in the collective psyche of all Bengalis from erstwhile East Bengal.

A translator is almost always a trans-creator. We all know that there are certain words and expressions and certain emotions which are exclusive. They form a part of a particular language or culture. As example, I could cite *abhiman*. *Abhiman* involves hurt, pain, sadness, anger, withdrawal and each of the emotions mentioned by me associated with *abhiman* are in turn associated with love, desire and longing. Is there an English word for it? Yet, *abhiman* is an emotion which is inseparable from Indian vernacular literature. In order to make up for this deficit, the translator has to recreate the original text for his target audience, fulfilling their horizon of expectations, "translating" and simultaneously "recreating" the text. Hence the term "trans-creation." "Translation is not a matter of words only: it is a matter of making intelligible a whole culture," said Anthony Burgess.

Sengupta has a sound knowledge of both the source language and the target language; in these cases, Bengali and English; and a sound comprehension of the different cultural background of the Western reader. Probably that is the reason why he has a prose prelude to his own poems. The prose introductions make his Western readers familiar with the many nuances of Indian life and culture.

Works Cited

Chakravertty, Tania. Book Review. *Desirous Water* by Sumita Nandi. *Contemporary Vibes*. Gurgaon, Haryana: The Poetry Society of India. April-June 2014, Vol. 9, Issue 35.

About Tania Chakravertty

Dr. Tania Chakravertty is an Assistant Professor and currently the Coordinator, post-graduate course, Department of English, Shri Shikshayatan College, Calcutta. Concurrently she is the Guest Lecturer in the Department of English, University of Calcutta since 2009 where she teaches selected texts in two papers: "Gender and Literature" and "American Literature" to the M.A. students. She was selected and she participated in a three-week US State-funded, academic group project, "Strengthening and Widening the Scope of American Studies: The U.S. Experience" in 2010 as a part of the International Visitor Leadership Program (IVLP). Tania contributes regularly to *The Statesman* [Kolkata edition]. She has contributed in Presidency Alumni Association's Autumn Annual [2014 - 15] — "Never Lonely and Never afraid": Love as a Panacea for Psychic Wounds in Hemingway's A Farewell to Arms. She got her paper ["Panchali's *Mahabharat*: A Feminist Re-reading in Chitra Banerjee Divakaruni's *The Palace of Illusions*] published in *Intertextuality: Poetics and Practice. A Collection of Critical Essays* [Radiance, Calcutta, 2013]. Her review of Ketaki Datta's *A Bird Alone* has been published in *Indian Literature* [Sahitya Akademi, Nov-Dec, 2009]. Tania's articles have appeared in several journals published by the departments of English in various Indian Universities.

An Afterthought

As a reader, editor and critic, I've always wanted to personally ask the poets themselves what they were thinking and what motivates them to write poetry. *Rhapsodies and Musings* allows me to do just that. Here Ketaki Datta examines the poetry of Sharmila Ray, and Tania Chakravertty looks at the poetry of Kiriti Sengupta. And they are asking the exact same questions I've always wanted to ask! Through them I gained a good understanding of these two well-renowned poets.

These explorations are written in a way that any English-reader will easily understand. And they offer more than just a surface look at these poets. Now when I read Ray and Sengupta I will have a solid base from which to understand their works. I firmly believe that we need more works like *Rhapsodies and Musings* so that we English-speakers can enjoy the ethereal, spiritual beauty of Indian English poetry — English-language poetry by the Bengali poets, to be precise!

Don Martin
July, 2015

[Don Martin is a bestselling author, editor, blogger and critic based in Tucson, Arizona.]